Unconditional
One Woman's Journey to Spiritual Freedom
LOVE

MARTICA L. OFFORD-SHERMAN

Copyright 2020 by Martica L. Offord-Sherman

All rights reserved. No part of this book may be reproduced in any form or by any electronic or mechanical means including information storage and retrieval systems, without permission in writing from the author. The only exception is by a reviewer, who may quote short excerpts in a review.

Printed in the United States of America

First Printing: April 2020

ISBN- 978-1-7346100-6-2

Contact Author Martica L. Offord-Sherman:
YHEC8NT@gmail.com
www.yhec8nt.com

CONTENTS

My Prayer for the Reader 5
Acknowledgements 7
Foreword 11
Preface 13
A Conversation with My Father as
His Favorite Daughter... 15
The Deep Things of God 17

Chapter 1: A Heart to Harvest.. 21
    A. The Unspoken Love 21
    B. Yes, this is a Matter of the Heart!........................... 23
    C. When the Heart Attacks... 23
    D. Love Stalled 24
    E. Love Undressed... 26
    F. Love's Pathway.. 27
Chapter 2: There is Growth in the Desert........................ 30
    A. Growing Through It... 30
    B. Desert Song 31
    C. Divine Romance.. 31
    D. Fruit from His Vineyard 32
    E. Tending Your Vineyard 33
Chapter 3: Undressed in the Vineyard 36
    A. Growing Strong in Him.. 36
    B. Divinely Undressed 36
    C. The Unpleasant Scent 38
    D. Naked While Covered 39
    E. The Twiggs 39
    F. Burning Bushes 41

Chapter 4: Transformation in the Vineyard 45
   A. A Fire in the Vineyard 45
   B. Intensity of the Fire 46
   C. Sifting Through the Ashes 46
   D. Seasoned by the Groundskeeper 47
   E. Set Apart.. 48

Chapter 5: Tending to the Vineyard............................... 51
   A. Tilling the Grounds 51
   B. Unwanted Objects in the Soil 52
   C. Infused Soil 53
   D. Firm Foundation 54

Chapter 6: The Groundskeeper 61
   A. Father Knows Best 61
   B. Festive Blend 63
   C. Dressing the Grounds 63
   D. Vineyard Décor 64

Chapter 7: Compression in the Vineyard 69
   A. The Refiner's Process 69
   B. Exposure to the Fire 70
   C. The Glass Window with the Reflective Mirror 72
   D. Purification 73

Chapter 8: New Wine 77
   A. Knowing His Plan 77
   B. Always in the Pruning Season 78
   C. A Washing Before the Reveal 79
   D. Take Notes for the Upkeep 81
   E. Dress for the Occasion 82

About the Author... 85

MY PRAYER FOR THE READER

My prayer for you would be that this book
exposes things you are looking to uncover in yourself, and
sets you on your own path. This book was created
just so you can discover your own truths
through your own experiences.

Acknowledgements

First, to give honor where honor is due! To the Lord of my life, Jesus Christ. Without Him, life would not be. But because He is my daily bread, I feast on His word and drink from His cup that never runs dry.

To my children, I had no idea that as a young girl praying for children, you would be one of my life's most significant accomplishments. Jeremy (my first born), you never knew this, but you gave me the will power to live in a cold world. I thanked God the day you were born. God spoke to me and gave me your name. I was obedient, and I know He was pleased. Kitona (my oldest daughter), I knew when I gave birth to you, my life had only just begun. You gave me the reason to become a woman and not stay a little girl. With you, I had to acquire morals and grow to become the young woman God created me to be. Kenneth Jr. (my baby boy), just like Jeremy, your birth helped me come out of a dark place. I began to speak, and God showed up! You gave me newness of life. Finally, to my baby girl Miyana, you are the flame in my fire. You gave me a reason to push on. Each of you is a special chamber in my heart, and I need all four chambers to function at my best. I love all of you.

To my parents Michael and Stella Offord, I thank God for bringing you both together in the 1970s to bring me here, so I may do my part in impacting the world. To my siblings, Michael and Sabrina, I also thank you. Watching both of you persevere during your life changes has helped me be a better person inside and out. To my nieces, Ashley and Michaela, thank you for reigniting the fire in my life.

To my legacy, Zayden K. Sherman and those to follow, the word of God says, a good man leaves an inheritance to his children's children. Everything I do, is done with you in mind.

To an extraordinary person (you know who you are), you had no idea this book was being written yet, I thank you so much for being you and giving me the reason for me to 'BE.' Since meeting you again, every day, I tell God He truly has a sense of humor, for I needed to grow up through the process. Thank you for being who and what you were meant to be in this season of my life. You stretch me spiritually, emotionally, and mentally. You push me in ways even I cannot explain. As a stone in my life, I'm thankful for your presence. Bricks only come in one uniformed shape and size, but rocks are rough around the edges, yet strong and solid in the right places. I will always be one of your biggest fans.

Louise and Isaiah Skinner, I truly thank God that he placed both of you in my life at the time He did. Your unconditional love has helped mold me to become the woman I am today. You came alongside me without any thought of yourselves and gave to me unselfishly. For this gift, I will be eternally grateful.

Thanks to my family on both sides.

Thank you to the men and women of God who have sown seeds and seasons into my life. May I bear the fruit of the journey that I have had with you as the great cloud of witnesses. The impact you all have made helped push me through the various channels of my life story to my purpose. Pastor Caleb B. Anderson of New Bethel WE in 5th Ward, TX, I truly thank
God for you from the depths of my soul. During my earlier years of walking with the Lord, you were always there for me as a pastor, brother, friend, and mentor. You impacted my life greatly and increased my desire to know and love the Lord more deeply. Thank you would never be enough. Dr. Patrick T. and Dr. Pamela Randolph, thank you for your impact on my life. I have the greatest respect for you and praise God for meeting you on my journey.

Foreword

Unconditional love and freedom are two of the most misunderstood and misused terms in the English language.

Growing up with cousins that total 43 grandchildren (22 of us being girls) my cousins and I each had the privilege of receiving truly unconditional love and freedom from our grandmother, Hattie Davis Rodriguez Smith. She allowed us the freedom to be ourselves, despite our parents, siblings, and all our flaws. I was her "favorite," and Martica was her "best friend." Each of us had our own place in her heart, and the bond of that love has withstood the test of time, distance, and life itself. We are forever connected by that love.

Martica's life has not been a crystal stair. However, in the words of Langston Hughes, Martica has courageously kept "climbing," reaching landings, and turning corners. She has persevered like a phoenix risen from the ashes and made a glorious exchange. Now she wears beauty instead of the ashes that sought to shroud her. She is anointed with the oil of joy and is clothed in the garment of praise.

No longer entrenched in toxic cycles, unable to distinguish between the good, bad, and the ugly, Martica candidly shares her trials and her triumphs.

This book is a must read for anyone, male or female, desiring true freedom. It is an open, honest, and forthright look into an often painful and arduous life path. Yet conceived in hope, it gestates faith and delivers the glorious joy of freedom.

Marilyn Y. Monroe, M.Ed.
Glorious Grand #1

Preface

Before you read this book, define love honestly in your own words. Now, think about what you were taught about love. As you begin to look at those signpost, speed bumps and detours in your life, remove what society says love is, and how it should be expressed. How close are you to reaching your destination? Somewhere there's a bush burning in your vineyard. Let's get you back on track.

Your journey begins here!

A Conversation with My Father as His Favorite Daughter

Lord, as we start this journey, I ask that You touch every heart that reads this book. I ask that You give them Your road map on how to love unconditionally. Lord, show them how You, the great Father, give love so freely. As You infiltrate every area of their lives, allow them to see You in them. Love is Your first commandment—to love unconditionally is Your greatest desire for us all. Let not one person reading this book walk away positively unchanged. Let this book stir up a desire to learn more of You, love others without resentment and correct any negative thinking about what love truly is.

The Deeper Things of God

Did you know I am the One who wrote
your story from the start?
Did you not think that I would complete the
chapters before your life would even begin?
Why would I put an audience before you
without giving you the script?
It is My Word that existed before you
that I engraved upon your lips.
You say you want to know Me.
You want the deeper things of Me!
Then why not embrace who you are in Me?
When I breathe on you as I did Adam, I imparted
into you everything you would need to be.
I AM, and ALL the deeper things of Me are already in you.
So why not look at you, for you are also looking at Me?
If it is the "Deeper Things of God" you seek.

Create in me a clean heart, O God, and renew a right *and* steadfast spirit within me.

Psalm 51:10 (AMP)

Unconditional Love

Chapter One

A Heart to Harvest

Everyone has an untold story that should be told. Pain hurts like a boulder sitting on your chest making it hard to breathe. What do you do with this pain? You find a solution to stop fighting the person or persons who hurt you by learning to allow our Creator to uncover each scar with His cream of healing. Each chapter will give you a piece of each scar that was healed in my life.

Imagine a love even the human mind cannot create. It is a love so beautiful even the human heart cannot beat fast enough to capture its rhythm. It has enough courage to look beyond people's faults and love them to see their needs. They need to believe they are not who the world depicted them to be. With spirits so unfulfilled, they need a love that restores them to their original intent.

 The Unspoken Love

We were taught to always show manners in and around others but never how to love unconditionally. We have to feel everything we go through, or we will not be able to allow ourselves to love as we were created to. People treat love like it's a virus not healthy for the mind, spirit, or soul. We can teach our children their names, colors, and addresses, but we are so afraid to teach them love is meant to cover others and not harm them. When we learn to love without conditions, sickness and disease will have no place in our bodies or minds. Love is such an unspoken word because the act is so unsure. Love in its purest form can cause a country to believe it can serve a nation, a parent to teach a child they are here with and for a purpose and a marriage to last far beyond an anniversary of years. It is human nature for us to seek after the things we long for the most.

We have an inclination that we don't need those things; when in fact, it is embedded in us to want it. It's how we inquire about it that hurts us the most. Love is the unspoken word that is so vaguely used without its true meaning. As we know, love is the giving of ourselves to someone unconditionally. But, do we really know this, or have we been so damaged that we forget our own value of what love truly is? Love is defined by every individual according to personal environment, not experience. If your environment never provided it, then you've never experienced it. You see, my experience is not your experience, yet my environment may have the same significance as yours.

I grew up with both parents in the household, and I learned love according to my environment. It was not until I tried to give what my environment taught me that I was able to experience what love was not. In watching my environment,

I was able to determine I did not want to love that way. My love would be different. But how could that be? I was not able to give what I could not understand or identify. It was just like trying to drive down a dark street without lights waiting to crash into something I could not see. This is the reason a lot of people are not reaching their full potential; they love from their environment and not from the heart of God. Your environment is what surrounds you and what you surround yourself with.

 ## Yes, this is a Matter of the Heart!

Remember, everything we do is a matter of the heart. I am not the judge or the jury—nor do I ever want to be. Our greatest happiness is within ourselves as long as we learn to love the way our Creator loved. Your love for others should never be a reflection of this world, but that of God's love towards us. Just as the heart beats, the love for others should be able to take on the formations of what flows from it. God's word speaks on the cleansing of the heart and the renewal of who we once were before the heart became reflective of its environment (Psalm 51:10).

 ## When the Heart Attacks

The heart, when untampered with, is a blank canvas awaiting the right strokes of the paintbrush to color it true. It is unexposed to the things each stroke of the brush can either paint, whether warm or cold. The heart pumps the blood that flows throughout the body. When the heart has been tainted or tampered with, inappropriate issues are uncovered, and life becomes emotional. Love is a language learned from your environment. It is not an overnight process, for if this were so, how could a person fall out of love with someone?

Love Stalled

Have you ever been driving somewhere, and you see the sign that says, "Stalled vehicle in a center lane"? Either there was a flat tire, they had run out of gas or the engine gave out; these things do not negate the promise. You have somewhere to be. In order for you to get there, you must take your eyes off the distractions. They are momentary. Just like that stalled vehicle, love has not reached its purpose or destination. Your flat tire could have been a broken relationship, failed business, unsuccessful event, or situations you had no control over. Most of us believe we are in control of everything, but if that were true, then why can we not control our destiny, feelings, emotions, and thoughts without someone telling us we can? I find it entertaining how we believe we have placed ourselves in certain situations only to find out it's a part of our purpose. Because of our narrow mindedness, we believe everything is all about us. Once again, you are in a stalled state because life did not pan out as you felt it should. Stalled is simply Stuck, Terrified, Apprehension, Lost, Limited, Empty, and Devastated by your own beliefs.

Stuck would be an area in your life in which you have personally decided to create your own life's manuscript without consulting the One who created and knows you best. You become someone other than yourself. You are unable to pick up the pieces from what you believed was love and move on to your next destination. Things happen in our lives causing our vehicle to become stuck on the road of life. Instead of moving forward, we start questioning ourselves wondering if we are moving in the right direction. Paralyzed by fear of failure, you may get stuck looking in the rearview mirror of life. If you don't have on your hazard lights during this season of your life, you will cause an accident.

Terrified is being trapped by what we thought should have been our future, but instead being comforted by complacency, resting on a temporary shoulder of the road. It feels right for a little while until you realized you need more than roadside assistance. What do you do? If you are like most of us, you contact family and friends because you are too afraid to ask for help from the One who created you and knows you best.

Apprehension is the fear of moving. Anxiety adds chaos to our life. It blurs our vision, clouds our judgment, and results in our inability to trust anyone around us, including ourselves. It deafens us with a barrage of voices which leaves us in a state of confusion.

Lost in oblivion, we are in a whirlwind of hopelessness. We don't have a clue of who we are or whose we are. When things don't line up the way we assumed our life should, we start seeking other outlets and avenues to help us to get back on the road. Those things can take us further away from our destination and cause a delay in our process. Notice, I said delay and not denial. Whenever you become lost, limitations can form.

Limited means you are confined and restricted by the inability to move forward. This is when frustration sets in and time slips into the future. It seems your desired result will not manifest, and this depletes you of empathy and compassion for others.

Empty is void, without form, full of darkness, anger, selfishness, and criticism. Your love tank is empty, you become susceptible to self-pity, victimized thinking, mental hoarding and toxicity.

Devastated and wrecked on the highway of life, you've been left feeling like a waste land, desolate, resentful, bamboozled and hoodwinked, believing no one is worthy of love including yourself. Now, you're infected, contagious, and acrimoniously spewing malice, or wallowing in the mire of low self-esteem.

 Love Undressed

Love undressed bares the nakedness of your soul to another who may be fully clad in his or her own misconceptions of what true love is. It's willing vulnerability. It risks, showing the scars of time, potholes of brokenness, and the detours of distractions in the excitement of meeting "the one." Ready for restoration, you cautiously re-enter the freeway of life.

Love's Pathway

No longer stalled, you are back on the highway with a full tank and equipped with the knowledge you have gained. You embark on this phase of the journey with your navigation system fully functional and giving clear directions. Now it's time to revisit your definition of love.

A Time of Reflection:

Now that you have come this far with me, has your definition of love changed? If not, then keep reading.

READER'S NOTES

_____
_____
_____
_____
_____
_____
_____
_____
_____
_____
_____
_____
_____
_____
_____
_____
_____

"And the Lord will continually guide you, And satisfy your soul in scorched *and* dry places, And give strength to your bones; And you will be like a watered garden, And like a spring of water whose waters do not fail.

Isaiah 58:11 (AMP)

Chapter Two

There is Growth in the Desert

 Growing Through It

As I was going through a divorce, I thought in my mind, it had destroyed my life, and the lives of my children. I was attached to a world I created without God in it. Sure, I would pray asking God to fix my marriage. The issue was the word "fix." I was asking God to fix something I created. I built an idol, a god, and a world in which I felt I had control. Looking back, I'm amazed I survived. I asked God to bless my mess, so I could remain comfortably in control. I just wanted the pain to stop and not be naked before people whom I believed loved me. But God said, "No," and that's when my growing season began.

As I grew through the desert, I was blessed with friends who refused to allow me to wear the beautiful mask I created. I had formed judgments within my heart against God, my husband, others and myself. I had to ask God to teach me how to forgive myself and learn how to love me. During this time,

I learned how things go according to God's plan and not my own. It taught me that asking God to put me back in control and restore a marriage He did not ordain was not His perfect will for me.

 ## Desert Song

As the songs of my life continue to play, at times, I see myself putting certain songs on repeat. My life slow dances with every note with my soul longing to see better, do better and be better. I wrestle within myself as to how I can hold a note to each song. With every chord that is struck, I listen to see which way I should move. With every melody, I search to find my line in each verse. It's not that my life is restless, just my feet, yet I cannot get tired of the dance. Sometimes the song is slow. Other times it is an up-tempo song. Either way, experience has made me the lead singer/performer of my own destiny. Life continues to play the instrumentals of each chapter of my life, so I can find my voice in the song. I'll close my eyes, so I can see the vision of the melody, the vibrations of the tunes, the colors of each note, and the fine-tuning of the hooks following each verse. As I warm up my vocal cords, I can see life's song come together and how just by singing my part, the song is so well put together.

 ## Divine Romance

As I emerged from the desert, a bud not fully matured, I realized my process was incomplete, and what I needed was to be divinely romanced by my Creator. The more time spent with Him, the more I begin to feel the rhythm of His heart for me.

His voice became soft whispers in the night as He serenated me with sweet songs of His love. Our hearts became in sync as I sat at His feet. He consummated His desire to make me whole in Him. He covered me by day with His wings of love and by night He saturated me with His kisses of peace. As I continued to spend time with Him, I begin to experience His love for me as if I were His only creation. I learned I was "God's Favorite Daughter"! United with Him as one, beautiful precious fruit came forth as an expression of His all-encompassing love for me.

Fruit from His Vineyard

One thing I've never want is something that didn't belong to me whether it be a job, a boyfriend, and especially a husband. The fruit that God produces in our separate vineyards belongs to each one of us. Like me, you have a vineyard where godly fruit is cultivated for you in your oneness in Him. God knows what you need. This is why as He divinely romances you, He is premating you with what you need to produce fruit. Like many people who are often drawn to wrong relationships you, too may have allowed the weeds of the world's system to come in and choke out the divine fruit that God has produced in your vineyard. This captivates your heart leading you to vineyards that are not yours. Enticed by a plate of happiness with fruit that will not satisfy, you find yourself empty. It is His divine love that produces what you need, and no other vineyard can produce that fruit. While it is physically appealing, it will not fill that spiritual void. The satisfaction is only temporary. For that reason, I am making this statement to you: "Let That Go!" Women, let go of that woman's boyfriend or husband! Men, let go of that man's girlfriend or wife!

Tending Your Vineyard

Now you've let go of that which didn't belong to you. With an unattended vineyard, you've allowed the world system's weeds to increase and over-run your garden. The work begins! You have to reconnect with the Father and allow Him to help you uproot the weeds through time alone with him. He meets you where you are, cleans you up and continues the process of loving you through healing. With the weeds now gone, He can love you freely, replanting and preparing you for your harvest.

A Point of Reflection:
Are you ready to begin again? Inhale. Take a deep breath. Now, exhale!

READER'S NOTES

"He cuts off every branch in me that bears no fruit, while every branch that does bear fruit he prunes[a] so that it will be even more fruitful."

John 15:2 (NIV)

Chapter Three

Undressed in the Vineyard

 ### Growing Strong in Him

The pruning season is a polishing within the vineyard. The ugliness of the healing is never fun. It cuts off the excess fruit that is not producing, and it stop the weeds from coming back. Hearing God's voice, seeking wise counsel, power journaling, mediation, and praise and worship are all His signpost letting you know that trusting Him is a process. So, ask God to cleanse you as you grow on this journey. Allow Him to bring what's inside of you out in areas He is cutting away, so more excellent fruit is produced. God had told me in our time alone it was time to clear out the vineyard for His work in me. He had to show me the weeds that had grown inside of me.

 ### Divinely Undressed

It wasn't until I said enough, when I become divinely undressed. I was the girl who went to church wanting to be the godly woman inside and out. I no longer wanted to cry myself to sleep at night. I wanted to stop playing church and be the church I had so desperately longed for. I needed to get past the weeds that had grown so wild in my own unkept vineyard. I had to realize I was her, the girl who went to church habitually. My intentions for a relationship with God were still unclear. I would hear God's voice saying, "Stop playing church, and date me." I would be there singing and praising while holding my pain like a blanket unwilling to let Him work on me. It became a blanket that keep me warm instead of hot for God. I had allowed my dress rehearsal to stay on repeat from what I tolerated to grow. I forgot to build a relationship with the Groundskeeper of my vineyard. In my time of playing church, God revealed to me there was a certain level of maturity I had to reach before I could become a godly woman. I was in a religion-ship when I needed to be in a relationship with him. I had to start dating Him and seeking His heart to love me as He saw me. God had to do a major overhaul within me to clean out the weeds of my leaving of my own vineyard to tend to another without seeking Him first. I wanted to be a godly woman with a personal relationship with God as my top priority. In doing so, I had to release the girl that went to church having goals of wanting to have a religion-ship with God, hoping to find a husband and wasting time creating a life without purpose. God showed me that a godly women's relationship with Him keeps her at peace. The relationship serves no other option for her because she's all about kingdom building and not building unhealthy relationships outside of Christ. Whether she is in a relationship or not, nothing takes precedence over her love for God.

The Unpleasant Scent

As God began to undress me layer by layer, I became stifled, overwhelmed, and uncertain about what to do next. Everything I knew started to sound muffled, become distasteful, unpleasant and muted. I felt as though I was without any direction in a whirlwind of emotions, floating on autopilot going in the wrong direction. The stench of my past relationships was on those layers. I had to stop masking them with "why" and put on the "why not" attire. Wrestling with internal thoughts of past relationships not panning out the way I'd hope made me rethink my previous choices in my vineyard. The stench of the previous hurt would attract that same hurt back to me. It was a fragrance which only those who sought after recognized. It would attract hurt like a buzzard eating after the death of a thing. I couldn't get out of my own head to be useful, not even for myself. I had to go back to the One who created and loved me first. He would help me find myself. He knew me better than I knew myself. When my experiences became my clothing, He started to peel them away. "Ouch, that hurts!" I would tell Him as He would address the hurt in my heart. Until one day He said, "Get up! Get out those clothes! Take a long hot bath! Wash your hair! Wash your face!" This journey had just begun. It was as if I were in the movie, "Invasion of the Body Snatchers" or "Aliens" in which the hurt had incubated my body by removing me from the One who loved me first. During this time, God never allowed others to see me uncovered. Still, no one knew during this season the overhaul that was taking place in my vineyard.

Naked While Covered

When hurt backed me into a corner, I had to either fight or cave in? Depending on the level of hurt, most of us will succumb to being prey to our predator. This happens simply from the unwillingness to let go of what holds us in fear. I also had one of the master manipulators called, **HURT** (Hiding Under Ridiculous Thoughts). God knows I was angry, hurt, and confused. I want to see those who hurt and wronged me be dealt with unjustly. I knew those thoughts were not of God, but how was I to feel at the time? Let's just be honest! I allowed this pain to happen, believing I was doing the right thing of forgiving them every time with the wrong intentions. I didn't see them hurting for the things and lies they had told. I saw them happy while I walked in the misery of losing things, I held close to my life. Life meant devoting my time and energy to people who, from the beginning, never cared for or loved me. I just wanted to scream, cry, hide, run, fight, and yell because I felt I had lost so much.

The Twiggs

After having a failed marriage, I was afraid to succeed at anything, let alone everything in life. I went through a period of identity theft. What noticed is that even while dating myself, I lied to myself. I was so afraid of commitment for fear of disappointment and hurt from others. So, I would begin to lie to myself out of that fear. I had to soon surrender and say, "Lord, I accept my assignment." I had to remember, identity theft is not just a credit report matter but a spiritual one also.

The enemy fights us daily for our identity. Knowing who we are is one part of our purpose and destiny. When we are having an identity crisis, we must be sure we know whose we are. It was when I began to recognize those "I don't belong here" moments, to notice something about the situation did not pan out to what I'd believe should be right.

As God would have it, He had to uproot the word **"REGRET"** from my vineyard. I had begun to become resentful of the hurt. I had to learn how not to regret my process and just enjoy the journey. I had to learn not to be "Remorseful" after losing people and things in my life from the pattern of planter boxes I had created. If they were there for a season, it was for a lesson or an experience needed for my next elevation. I had to learn how to continue to give God my "Emotions," so I would stay out of my feelings and not hoard the pain from something not working. I also had to learn if I did not allow God to help me with my emotions, it would cause me to walk around with a "Grudge" towards someone who was not against me. God was using this situation to deliver me. "Rebellion," according to God, is witchcraft. I was fighting against the things that hurt me when I should have been asking God what I was to have learned from it. I would just shut down and deal with it later when later was not the answer. It is when I knew I had a greater purpose than the things that were trying to distract me from my calling. "Emptiness" is what I would feel because I had nothing to build me back up, which is what I thought. I learned how much God loved me when I could talk to him and get a response. At that moment, I realized I was so full; it was destined for me to share my testimony with others.

"Tormented" is what I felt when I allowed my emotions to surface. Instead of letting those things show me what God was cleaning up in me, I aborted the process. I later learned that those things that hurt me the most were God's way of letting me know that He was the only one who can fix it. I had to find joy in the process.

 Burning Bushes

I wasn't enjoying life. Clothed in my multicolored blankets of hurt, I wanted to manipulate my situations just to stay covered. I started searching for reasons to stay in the weeds, until one day, I had to walk in my own truths. My blanket which kept me warm was now on fire. It wasn't the people or the things that were the problems but how I responded and handled the people and things.

A Point of Reflection:
Are you ready for the Refiner's fire?
The Groundskeeper is ready to start the landscaping.

READER'S NOTES

_____
_____
_____
_____
_____
_____
_____
_____
_____
_____
_____
_____
_____
_____
_____
_____
_____
_____
_____

"Everything that can stand fire, you shall pass through fire, and it shall be clean. Nevertheless, it shall also be purified with the water of purification [to remove its impurity]; and all that cannot stand fire [such as fabrics] you shall pass through water."

Numbers 31:23 (AMP)

Martica L. Offord-Sherman

Chapter Four

Transformation in the Vineyard

 A Fire in the Vineyard

As God began to work on me from the inside, I knew I would be exposed without being covered. I wanted to be open but safe without revealing my feelings and emotions. Not wanting to uncover the hurt that festered so deep inside of me, I would shut down. This meant I had to give Him everything. I had to give Him total control. Since I was exposed, thoughts in my head begin telling me things that were not true about me. Those silent whispers told me things like, "You're not worth it. They never liked you anyway, and they were only there to play games with your heart." It was those thoughts while having to get to know who I truly was that caused the fire in my vineyard. As I gave Him all of layers I had so comfortably wrapped myself in year after year, the intensity of the fire started to burn in other areas I thought were not affected. I had to be open, ready and willing to be whom and what I was created to be throughout my journey here on the earth. The best thing I've learned is, whatever someone does to me, they are doing this to God as long as I abide in Him. God unraveling of the mess I had created opened the doorway to my healing.

 ## Intensity of the Fire

The more I drew closer to God the intensity of the fire burned impurities. I had to learn while developing in the vineyard when I step out, I must represent Him well. During my time of transformation, I had to stay "CLASSY." I had to be "Careful" of who I allowed in my life, speak into my life and connect to my purpose. I was once "Loyal" by default but had to learn my loyalty was only to Him. I had to become "Available" to love as God has instructed me to, which is unconditional. "Submission" did not mean to be taken for granted but to enhance what God has purposed in me to give as He instructed. Being "Steadfast" was not just for me but for Him, so I must stay intimate in my relationship and time with God in prayer, praise, and worship. Speaking life every day as if He's my journal of love letters just like the Book of Solomon. As the smoke cleared and as the vineyard was surveyed, the Groundskeeper began to mark new grounds for planting.

 ## Sifting Through the Ashes

Have you ever picked up dirt and opened your hand? As the dirt begins to fall from your hand, the amount you picked up begins to decrease? I considered this as the ashes of my past, the rubble from the fire and the beauty of which God was doing in my vineyard. I asked God to show me Him in everything I endured. Have you ever prayed, and after prayer, just felt the ire and heavy feelings afterwards? Then those things that you prayed against still bother you? Just mere residue. The fire has burned out, smoke fills the air, the ground is covered in soot and the cleanup begins. What God has planted still remains.

 Seasoned by the Groundskeeper

As my conversations with Him got real, my cries came from a deep place, and the laughter straight from the gut. It was during those quiet times my prayers were no longer about me. My tears felt like fire, and my prayers felt so deep I became spiritually separated from everything around me. As the Groundskeeper tended to those unfruitful areas of my vineyard, I had to keep in mind that every seed He planted had my unique coating on it. The coating became a part of the soil within my vineyard by seasoning the grounds while the Groundskeeper kept revealing Himself to me. It was in those separation times God provided revelation of the innermost parts of my life. He uprooted and replanted me in His fertile grounds to grow in the things of Him. He knew my heart's desires, yet He made my desire for what He wanted so appealing that my roots dug deeper for more of Him. Our relationship changed from religion-ship until I would always tell Him He had a serious sense of humor with me. He would show me something, and I would try not to laugh, but in Him is where I truly found joy.

 Set Apart

I never understood what it meant to be single. As a single woman and mom, now I'm enjoying life. Don't get me wrong; I wrestle with crazy thoughts like, "Yeah, but you are alone!" That may be so, but I'm not lonely. For those of us who were once married, in relationships or just involved, not having someone in your presence feels different, but it's a time to learn more about yourself. Getting to know the real you if you never knew who that person was should become priority. I'm talking about the you behind closed doors no one else knows. Allow me to set the table for you. If you have dirty dishes in the sink, would you go into the kitchen and reuse a dirty plate to eat on? No, it will make you sick. So why would you want God to put that nasty thing back into your life without cleaning it up to His perfection and replacing the dinnerware with something better? The Groundskeeper will wash you clean!

Time of Reflection:
Are you ready for the cleanup?
The match is being lit, and there is no turning back.

READER'S NOTES
_____
_____
_____
_____
_____
_____
_____
_____
_____
_____
_____
_____
_____
_____
_____
_____
_____
_____
_____

Martica L. Offord-Sherman

I planted the seed, Apollos watered it,
but God has been making it grow.

1 Corinthians 3:6 (NIV)

Chapter Five

Tending to the Vineyard

 Tilling the Grounds

As God continued to till the soil of my vineyard, every part of my life was going through its own transformation process. I found myself trying to understand my own thoughts, dreams and lessons to be learned within them, whether good or bad. Wondering if the path I had chosen was really the one I needed to be on. While searching for an answer and walking through my healing process, relationship frustration started to rear its head. The residue of my past was trying to regrow as weeds in my future. Giving up total control to HIM (Holy-one Inside Me) would allow Him to perfect those things trying to rehash themselves. God never said these things would not happen, but He did tell me how I could handle them. It is in those quiet times of meditation while talking to God, He would give me a level of maturity according to my faith in Him. I began to seek Him with an urgency and a thrust only He could fulfill. Because I had an intimate relationship with him far beyond my understanding, my eyes became enlightened. My desire became a real hunger for Him, not just in lip service. I had had to learn my desires needed to line up with His desire for me. When we are infants in the Lord, our focus isn't on what God wants. It's usually on what our flesh wants. My desperation for Him was not out of helplessness but humility.

Unwanted Objects in the Soil

There's something about the word "Desire." Desire can be a need or a want. It is better to need than to want. Just as with any great groundskeeper, tilling the soil results in the removal of weeds, undesirable root, rocks and insects. Not every rock and insect are bad. Some are in place to help with the journey. Just as with any great groundskeeper, God had to show me who would stay and who would go. I called them all my "Season Sowers." I looked back at my marriage, and I saw the lesson I learned had nothing to do with him yet everything to do with me. I recall looking at many marriages and saying to myself, "That is not how I want my marriage to be." I kept putting unwanted objects in my vineyard. Somehow, things I saw but didn't wanted ended up planted in my soil. I didn't want them, but I would allow them to stay. When God intervened to clean up the soil, the undesirable roots were deep and sucking the life out of me, so He had to set things on fire to burn the impurities. The nights I cried with tears so toxic, they would burn my eyes and skin. The nights I would be alone holding my pillows so tight praying to get through the night without crying myself to sleep. I just wanted the stripping of the layers to stop although it felt good after it was revealed.

 Infused Soil

As the grounds of my vineyard were being tilled and fertilized, God began to infuse the soil with dreams and visions of His promises for my life. As He would only give me just a glimpse into what was going to happen, my impatience started to get the best of me. Excited about what I was seeing, I became numb to the stripping of the layers. I wanted to stand up and run before time just to get the things I saw. However, I realized that being impatient got me into trouble, especially during a time I wanted help with the outcome. Because of my impatience, the result of my past hurts and brokenness became the weeds in my vineyard. I ran to tend to some else's vineyard because I thought it looked and smelled nice. I didn't take into account signs, such as the way it talked to me, the way it treated me, and the way it took from me. I never tried to change the scenery. I just liked the way things perceived to be. I didn't have to do any work. I just had to look the part. As I took on more layers of living a lifestyle I was not afraid to live. I could be someone I was not as the weeds made me feel invincible. Oh, how God protected me during that season! I allowed the weeds, undesirable roots, rocks and insects to become so attached that it prohibited me from becoming what God would have me to become in that season. I could not hear Him clearly to do all that He would have wanted me to do even if I tried. This included waiting on His promise for the mate He had for me. I had to allow

God to infuse my soil as He willed. Take this lesson from me: while waiting for your "God thing," you should be tentative, teachable and submissive to the Lord, His ways and His path for your life. You have to watch what comes out of your mouth during your tilling season. I had to truly learn how to shut my mouth, forgive without reacting and spend time with God as He help me to grow in this process.

Firm Foundation

There's a process of healing, which may take baby steps just as the growing process of a plant. Instead of a plant I will walk you through my process of healing as it was similar to the human's gradual progress from lifting the head, rolling over, scooting, crawling, pulling up, stumbling, and then to finally walking. While being single, there are stages that you may see yourself grow through. The word single is not defined by your relationship status. You can be separated, independent of others, yet in a good and godly way. In return, God nurtures, grows, leads, and elevates you. Let's take a look at each of these stages:

Lifting your head (the beginning stage):
Just as with infants or newborn babies, during the early stages of their infancy, they want to lift up their heads to see what is going on around them even though they don't have 20/20 vision. Their eyesight is blurry, yet they can see distorted images. This was a stage in which I wanted to see what God was doing in my life while working in my vineyard. I wanted

to see the finished work although I could not see past the smoke and ashes. I had to depend on Him being my five senses of touch, smell, tasting, hearing and seeing. Through the fire my senses had to be renewed.

Rolling over (the post beginning stage):
I call this the audio stage. This is where the baby hears a noise and is trying to figure out exactly where the sound is coming from. They start moving in different directions to try to locate the sound. Have you ever gotten to this stage of wanting to know how to access God's voice? Do you still want to know where the noises are coming from? Allow God to be your guide. This stage was just like the others. I had to continue to learn to trust Him in everything. I still had the scales on my ears of my past. Too afraid to be hurt and allow anyone to know me, I was still that little girl who felt unprotected. I was the little girl who had her voice taken before she could even talk. I continued growing as the young girl who lost her trust in people, so she prayed to have children to love her. I lived as the young woman who was treated as a second hand by some people and then turned down by everyone else. I existed as the woman who got married only to be in a marriage by herself because she felt she had no control.

Scooting (the stage where you are working on getting up):
When you are single, you go from the visual part (which is the lifting of your head) to see what's going on around you. All of a sudden, something catches your eye. It actually mesmerizes you. You can't seem to take your eyes off of it. Your inquisitive nature causes you to want to get closer. This is also

the time you need to get closer to God, which is exactly what I did. At this point I began to dig deeper inside of myself only to realize I had paralyzed my life. I began to cry out to God in worship, reading, writing and music. I would journal our conversations. I would write poetry and songs to Him. I had to get to Him!

Crawling (the stage where you are making moves towards healing):
Sometimes, in the scooting stage, you may bump into something or someone that causes you pain. Well, you've been hurt before, and so have I, but this is the stage where you have to know precisely which direction you are going. Don't allow your past hurts to detour you from God's original intent for a godly relationship. This is the stage where you move forward towards the healing stage. Prayer became my best friend. I grew up as an intercessor. Conversations with my Grandma Madear (Hattie) would always put me back on track with God. It was like she would sense when I would see visions and have dreams. While, you can say God used her to cultivate my gift, it was actually in my crawling stage my relationship with God became my main source of strength. I stayed at this stage for quite some time. It's okay. Just don't live there. I had to learn how to crawl again, get back up on my feet, and see the people in my past life the way God sees them.

Pulling up (the stage where you see yourself through God's eyes):
Now, the pulling up stage is something very different. For over 20 years, I lived in a bubble—a bubble I had created. It didn't allow anyone else close to me because I didn't want them to hurt me. After six years of being inside of that bub-

ble, it took someone different to show me that life was so much more than what I had closed myself from. This person had me questioning God. What was His plan? I started removing pieces of the bubble daily with God's word. This person wanted nothing from me like everyone else from my past. I was able to see the person God created with flaws and all. I was able to love who I was and not be ashamed of my uniqueness because this person was unique as well. It felt good to "pull up" shaky legs and all.

Stumbling (the stage where you fall back a little):
In this stage, you realize you're human, and falling again is a strong possibility because of it. But God! His grace and mercy catches us like Jesus caught Peter when he attempted to walk on water. God does not condemn us because of our faulty nature. For years, I hid within the walls of the local church where my pain and I co-existed. There was no room for God. Even though I visited Him regularly. He eventually told me to "stop playing church." I had to realize that only God had the healing power to erase my pain. I was keeping Him on the outside. There was false security in the bubble I created for myself. It wasn't until I found the courage, like Peter, to take a step forward in faith, bursting the bubble, that I gained access to God's healing. I fell, but God helped me up. Falling does not negate the love God has for you. You will stumble. Just don't live there.

Walking (the healing stage):
The walking stage is the one stage where all of us should purpose to be. It is here where we seek and hear God. In the

book of Genesis, God and Adam communicated daily in the garden by simply walking around and having a conversation with each other. They were able to talk so freely and so open about everything; a son can have this kind of relationship with his Father, and that's love. When you learn to walk it becomes an individual relationship with God. It is being able to walk side-by-side in the likeness of Him. When you are walking with God, talking with Him, you should be listening as He tells you His purpose for your life. Don't be afraid to walk with the Creator. He sees you in His image.

Time of Reflection:
Are you ready for the upgrade? It does come with a price. The best fertilizer is never cheap.

READER'S NOTES

"I am the vine; you are the branches. If you remain in me and I in you, you will bear much fruit; apart from me you can do nothing.

John 15:5 (NIV)

Chapter Six

The Groundskeeper

 Father Knows Best

I had to allow God to move me from the seasons of wanting to be in a relationship, married, loved, loyal, and committed to surrendering my thoughts and feelings to Him. I walked in disappointment, hurt, frustration, and anger only to realize the Groundskeeper needed to come in and uproot bitterness and fertilize with His love and forgiveness. I had to learn the Dis-Appoint-Ments I had endured were Not-A-Point-Meant for me to connect to in those seasons. While living a life of surrender, He gave me an appetite for the new things of Him, which included new look on life, a new relationship and not religion-ship with Him. I had to constantly release the new things God gave me. I felt just like the kid, when my parent gave me something then said to give it back until I could learn to appreciate it. I was emotional each time. In my seasons of learning how my Father knew what was best for me, my days became my nights, and my nights became my days.

I know this sounds so reversed, but this is how He had to work with me. He had to take me backwards, so that I could see more clearly the direction I was going. I would ask Him, "How can you give me something and then say surrender it daily?" The Father did this to make sure I didn't have another god before Him.

That's when God spoke to me and said, "BE!" As I stated before, when God talks to me, He breaks words down into acronyms for me. The word "BE" can be whatever revelation God gives. He told me to not be anxious but become "Balanced"—not to be eager to make things happen in my life but be "Everything" He created in me. Don't get me wrong; it was not always easy. My focus became intentional and allowed Him to take center as I evolved. I had no time to lose heart over things not moving at the pace I wanted them to. Learning how to "BE" was not for that person. It is always for you. Even during hardships, loss, and disappointments I had to learn how to "**BE**" (Balanced in Everything). I had to allow God to have total control in directing me. It's like the saying, "We want what we want when we want it." But, if we rush it to fruition before it's time when it is not ready, it could be detrimental to our journey. The Groundskeeper taught me how to take control of my thoughts through the daily quoting of His Word. Two of the main scriptures, both of which became part of my favorites, were Philippians 2:5 and II Corinthians 10:5, allowing me to "BE" without judging others.

Festive Blend

Now, many of you may not agree, understand, or appreciate this part of the book because the word "Forgiveness" is so foreign to you. I recall a conversation I had about forgiving and forgetting. We have to touch on this topic because in order to love, we must forgive and forget. I had to learn that forgetting is not for that person but for my healing. Forgetting is just to make sure I am not holding that incident in my heart. When I walked around with those past thoughts and hurts, I carried that baggage into every relationship as a religious cloth of hurt. In the renewing of my mind, forgiveness and forgetting became the festive blend of aroma the Groundskeeper used to recognize me. Those feelings and thoughts that held me captive were affecting me personally. Holding those thoughts of what someone did to me or didn't do was emotionally draining and unhealthy. Having the mindset that everyone is not the same and should not be treated the same was one of my hardest hurdles. If God could forgive me and forget what I had done, then why couldn't I do the same of people? God began to festively blend the soils of my hurts and pains so I could See the offense was not towards me. When I learned how to forget, it freed me up of holding in as well as holding on to things I had no control over. Now, I could give them to the one who is at war for me.

 Dressing the Grounds

In this forgiveness, I was able to acquire love in the right way. The Groundskeeper would take His time with me even in the most tender moments with His presence through song, word and visions. I began to see the fresh new look God was doing in me. I was able to partake in the ceremony of seeing the new grounds of my vineyard as His love became such a strong fragrance during our time alone. My tears fertilized the soil, and my prayers continued to till the grounds for preparation of my new reveal. I learned to appreciate people differently in how they interacted with me. I can now tell season sowers from the transients. I recognize those who come to water from those who come to view, pluck-up and vandalize the grounds. There is no need to pick up remnants left behind, for they all serve a purpose. But now there is a limit to the stay. The grounds had matured, and growth had taken place.

 **Vineyard Décor**

Each piece has been placed to reflect the work the Groundskeeper has done during my journey. There were things I was afraid to be exposed until He said to me, "Who told you to pick up the pieces? You're not the Groundskeeper! Why are you trying to pick up the pieces that you cannot put back together? You could not begin to know how to place each piece in its place." To Him, the things that happened in my vineyard were as mosaic tiles. Each piece had a uniqueness in its design just to be placed in a specific spot. Every day with each moment of life as a piece chipped off, the Groundskeeper would place it back where He intended for it to go. The pain, that broken marriage, that broken relationship, that broken bone, and even that broken ministry served a purpose in my vineyard. Look at the keyword, "broken"!

Everything broken doesn't have to be fixed. It is in that brokenness the unfinished work is being crafted with purpose for A "Master's Piece"!

Time of Reflection:
Are you ready for the reconstruction?
The vineyard is coming along, and you are doing great.

READER'S NOTES

"There is no fear in love, but perfect love casteth out fear: because fear hath torment. He that feareth is not made perfect in love."

1 John 4:18 (KJV)

Martica L. Offord-Sherman

Chapter Seven

Compression in the Vineyard

 The Refiner's Process

While under reconstruction, lots of things I deemed important were removed as God said they had served their purpose. I didn't fully understand what He meant until one day while sitting in the tub, God took me through Jesus' total transition from the love to the rejection In a brief moment I was able to feel the burning of compassion after asking what "Love" truly was. From that day I knew it was something I could not give selfishly. I found myself weeping uncontrollably. While experiencing Him my family was in the house with me, but no one heard me. Before this encounter, I had yet to experience Him through my lip service of religion. He showed me when you love someone, you experience them. The more I experienced Him the more things started to fall off. As I drew closer to the fire, the more I became consumed, and the less I felt the burn. Freedom became my quest.

Exposure to the Fire

To experience the Groundskeeper of your vineyard is to be selfless yet selfish through intoxication of Him. Breathing His fragrance is a fire so contained the only thing burning is impurities from your soil. I was afraid of being exposed. I forgot in my experiencing Him I was protected. Exposure is not a bad thing. We become afraid of the unknown—the unknown of being exposed to others when it is in our true openness we become selfless and selfish at the same time—selfless in transparency yet selfish in wanting to experience Him more. True exposure does not make us weak; it is an indication of our great inner strength. We can show strangers our outer shell of appearance while refusing to invite them into our journey for fear of exposure. We become selfish by being unwilling to take them in for the sake of hiding what they may be able to help us heal. Exposure only becomes harmful when we lose focus on why it is being done. In January 2015, I can remember my youngest daughter saying to me, "Mom, when I go off to college, you are going to meet someone and fall in love again." Of course, I laughed because I didn't want to bring my exposed vineyard into a new relationship. The person she spoke of did not deserve to be exposed to my reflective image of a destroyed heart willing to heal yet not willing to love again.

After she told me this, I had an encounter with God to confirm what she had said about a relationship with someone. This person and I would sharpen each other because of our experiences. Of course, our vineyard experience may have not been the same, but it would tell our story of healing. This person and I would have both gone through some of the similar things in life , and through our process, would be able to help others. So, I had to surrender learning how to use the heart muscle again. I had to remember that it would take time and not to rush it. I treated it like a deep breathing exercise. As I took my focus off wanting to see how far along my vineyards process had come and continued to step into the fire, God and His humor happened.

I can remember asking God for a very long time about a person who came into my life unexpectedly. Why was anyone here? Where did this person come from? I began to put up this wall for fear of being open. very time I would feel a certain way, I would shut down emotionally and backup to avoid getting hurt. I didn't want to consider anyone's past or present condition. Understanding they had a past they may not want to let it go to be exposed and some of their past may not want to let them go. Please understand, we all have a past. The Groundskeeper is there to expose it to us only for cleanup. He is not concerned about our past but the part of our past we never dealt with. Allow Him to expose it to the fire for burning. This is for male and female when I say, "The skeletons in your closet still live!" They are just resting until you show interest elsewhere, so they can jump out to expose what you think you are hiding. The Groundskeeper can show you how to deal with them before you deal with something or someone else, and once burned, they cannot return. So, give them an exposure party and a proper burial, so they can move on. If not given a proper burial and left unattended, the stench becomes a fragrance only the Groundskeeper can replace. The outcome will be great, yet the process will take longer than needed.

The Glass Window with the Reflective Mirror

Let me be honest. The more God exposed me, my own eyes of judgment for others became my reflection of myself. I was that glass window with a reflective mirror. I called myself a Christian through religion, but my walk did not always reflect Christian values. I was willing to share and show my own failures but at a limit. In having my own faults, I still wanted control as I was willing to forgive my ex-husband. He could be forgiven as I was willing to let him go when he was not willing to submit to me, but that was not the order of God. God began to work on me. Then I realized I was not ready to have him back as my husband again or any man at that point. I became a product of my pain. I had friends of the male gender I would talk to and one who I was physical with only to fulfill my flesh. It was not a need but a want. I had been without a man in my life for a long period before, so I had no excuse. I cannot and will not use the excuse of his unfaithfulness to justify my actions. That would be a lie of Satan. I DIDN'T have to do what I thought, believed or felt that he was doing. If I did, then that meant I did not love myself either. When I came to myself like the prodigal son, I chose to do things God's way and walked away from every relationship until I could heal in my vineyard. The Groundskeeper told me to date Him as He would change the window in which I saw love.

As I began to allow God's healing to take place in my mind, heart and soul, I said no more to pleasuring my flesh. I made up my mind that there would be no more walking around as if nothing was wrong—as if I didn't have fears, hurts, desires and unfulfilled emotional needs. I wasn't ready to remarry. My soil was toxic from the skeletons I never dealt with. I had inhaled the fragrance and become numb. I needed the Groundskeeper to come in and do a major overhaul in my vineyard. This was something I never experienced before. Now without a relationship for six years, I had to allow His unconditional love to heal me before I could give love to someone else. I had to learn not just how to live but to love unconditionally. Learning to love unconditionally is so freeing. It takes on a different form that truly allows you to recognize a maturity only God can give you to love other people. This love should be so transparent, you only see the Groundskeeper and not the person. True love is iridescent and radiant, drawing you to inspect its beauty. It is reflective of everything God created yet so transparent that no one should have to do anything to inquire or look for. Genuine and real love can take the coldest heart and make it beat again. The particles of what is left after giving love is what the Groundskeeper increases.

 **Purification**

He not only wants your good days but your bad days as well. As the Groundskeeper sifts through the fruit of your vineyard to find the best to sell at the market, He cuts down the dried-out weeds, removes rocks that have served their purpose, and uses His Word as a pesticide for poisoning insects and vineyard devouring pests to assure nothing takes away the value of His crops. You cannot give God junk and leftovers and not expect Him to restore it with His best. He can make your past hurts your biggest miracle. As the Groundskeeper gives you a glimpse into the conversations you and God once had in the garden before the fall of man, He has to make room by purifying your vineyard. We are always in the purification cycle of our journey. Before we can be poured into new wineskin, the crushing, shaping, molding and compression of our vineyard preordains and predestines us before the stamp of approval is given. Although we are yet a finished product in the Lord, we are complete in Him. He sees the finished work, and to Him,

it is well worth the process.

Time of Reflection:

Are you ready for the reveal? You cannot go back into your vineyard in old clothing. It's time for new dressings.

READER'S NOTES
_____
_____
_____
_____
_____
_____
_____
_____
_____
_____
_____
_____
_____
_____
_____
_____
_____
_____
_____

"Inside I am like bottled-up wine,
like new wineskins ready to burst."

Job 32:19 (NIV)

Chapter Eight
New Wine

 ### Knowing His Plan

One I was driving to California to pick up my oldest daughter from college. It was her freshman year. She had no idea how much had changed within that year for me. As I was driving through Arizona, I began to talk to the Lord as I do daily. While talking to the Lord, He began to show me things my broken heart and draining mind could not fully understand. As we were driving through the mountains, He changed my view of sights such as the wondrous colors of dirt, the shapes of the mountains, and the atmosphere. As I looked upon what was surrounding me, I noticed how they looked like people lying on their backs with their mouths wide open. Each mountain was so uniquely shaped. Before I could even ask, the Lord spoke to me saying, "See those mountains? See how I masterfully decorated them? They praise me without asking. They have a relationship with me as I dress them for every occasion, every season and every journey." As He and I began to walk my vineyard, He brought me back to a previous conversation to which He confirmed to me again about trees. Trees start as seeds planted taking root in the soil it is buried in. The soil has to be prepared in order for the seed to produce its kind. My soil was damaged. Hard in some places. Untreated in others. Clay in some spots and shallow in others. I forgot about conversing with the Groundskeeper about my vineyard. I was busy tending to someone else's fruit. Soon, I began to see that I wasn't maintaining my soil the way He instructed me at the age of 14 when I first experienced Him. I knew His plan when I encountered Him after trying to take my life. One cold night in a psychiatric ward, I cried out to God with everything in me for Him to come see me. Let's just say, I never had to take any medications. It was then in my vineyard I would meet the Groundskeeper and learn of His plan for me.

Always in the Pruning Season

Learning His plan didn't just stop there. I had to understand that pruning season is a continual thing. Throughout my life I had to allow the Groundskeeper to landscape my vineyard. Pruning is not always a bad thing. As I began to grow in Him, relate to Him, allow Him to see me intimately was when pruning became empowering. At that point I had to stop, look at my vineyard and address the Groundskeeper for never leaving me uncovered. I was able to return to my first love, learning His Plan and letting go of the twigs that had me so deeply trapped in trying to be someone I was not. I am His child. He is my Father. The Father and I are one, but there's only one Father. His love is the best. With love being an action word, He committed the ultimate act of love by speaking you into existence, creating all other things to complement your existence, while instructing you how to live a life pleasing to Him. So why not consult with Him about His plan for you? Letting go of things held dear to you may seem hard, yet grabbing hold to Him is much better. This is a part of pruning. There should not be a day that goes by you are not in His presence to experience Him.

When you love someone, you want that person to be around to learn of his or her thoughts and ways. You want that person to love you back the same. Believe me, the only person who can do this and do it in the right way is the Groundskeeper Himself. Just because you think He's not tangible does not mean He cannot love you. He is just as real as an actual human being sitting in front of you. You may not be able to see Him physically, but He does exist.

A Washing Before the Reveal

My quiet times are for pruning and preparation. A time of breaking ground, burning, tilling, cleaning, refining, purification, and compression was necessary before the Groundskeeper could poured me into my new season and take my life to another level in Him. He is such a gentleman, even when we are so quick to push Him off for the flesh of another for temporary satisfaction. He never devalues us. He spoke to me and said, "Love me more than you loved your ex-husband." At first, I did not understand. I wanted to be all spiritual. Again, my vineyard was of religion and not relationship. When the Groundskeeper spoke to me about my divorce, I did not know what He was preparing me for next. All I know is, I had to love him more to get through the next stages of my life. No, it was not easy. It was after the pruning the washing of my vineyard became evident. The Groundskeeper started pressure washing the stands that held up my vines, detailing the branches and scrubbing the roots within my soil. He started with the things closest to me first. My children told me about how overcommitted I had become to hide the mess in my vineyard. Avoiding and involved in everything, my trust was only in the things I did. I became so involved until I wasn't available in my own life. I praised and worship, attended prayer intercession, missionary and anything else I could do assuming that was showing God I could love. I was really masking a pain that was going to hit me much harder than a tsunami of circumstances.

I went from being married to being someone I didn't know. I made being married my identity. The Groundskeeper showed me everything about myself. You see, my ex-husband was not a bad person, for we are not bad people. I was not a part of his vineyard. I was out of place. I had many chances of leaving before things got too far off course, but I didn't know how to "BE." So, I failed. Strangely, I was okay with failure. I was not my best self in the relationship. I could not give anyone what I did not have to give out. After I embraced the failure, I once again found my vineyard. I found out why God said what He said to me about "loving Him more than I loved my ex-husband." Now, don't get me wrong, this was in no way stated negatively. God was redirecting my focus on loving

Him, which would keep me from becoming bitter about what happened. I had to learn how to date God, which was a form of dating myself. Dating God is not what most people would think, but it is everything a believer needs. It teaches you how to love and handle relationships on another level. When God pursues you, your carnal mind cannot understand the things your spirit is receiving, so it has to leave. My language of conversation had to change with Him. I had to continue to allow my roots to dig deeper in His soil of fertilization as the water began to reside in my vineyard to reveal more of His plans.

Take Notes for the Upkeep

Freedom became my goal along with inner peace. We have the best manuscript for our vineyard in two places, His Word and our relationship with Him. Have you ever found yourself in a conversation with God only for Him to remind you of His way and not yours? I have plenty of times. Not fully understanding the word "Restoration" can delay your outcome. One day while riding in my truck and talking to God, He reminded me that when He restores a thing, there's no pain involved. There may be some stretching and discomfort, but when the finished product is presented, no one would ever know what happened except you, God and the one He personally designed for you. When the Groundskeeper dresses you, you begin to acknowledge His love which takes intimacy with Him to another level. Far beyond the fleshly definition, this is an intimacy that goes so deep your spirit is satisfied even when nothing else is. To be spiritually satisfied may sound spooky to those who do not understand spiritual things. God's words even say do not speak spiritual things to the foolish, for they will not understand them. The Groundskeeper knew I wasn't foolish but hungry for something He had. So I began to take notes which most say journal. I did this daily during my times of meditation. I learned mediation is intimacy with the Groundskeeper. I got quiet, listened to His voice, and wrote the love notes He gave me in that still small voice. I created a meditation playlist according to what He gave me to listen to in the season of my vineyard. I realized every song, thought written and time of travel all were a part of my preparation in my vineyard.

 Dress for the Occasion

As I became more in tuned with the melody of His heartbeat, the garments He dressed me in became so transparent. My vineyard is so beautifully decorated, and my fragrance is unique for His nostrils. The fragrance given to me became my attraction to those who needed what I had in my vineyard at its appointed time to blossom. So, when you see me smiling, laughing, and enjoying life, just remember the Groundskeeper dressed me in His Plan. I know my purpose! I'm deeply planted in my vineyard, and I intend to continue its upkeep with the Groundskeeper always before me. So, I say to you, "'Y HE C8NT' do the same for you?"

Have fun in your new vineyard!!!

Time of Reflection:

Are you refreshed? The vineyard is open for viewing. Just don't let the transients stay too long. Don't forget to journal daily.

READER'S NOTES

Martica L. Offord-Sherman

About the Author

The pursuit of freedom is an age-old quest of many a weary traveler. However, each journey is significant because it contributes to humanity's liturgy of liberty. Martica L. Offord-Sherman's journey, though unique to her experience, is a universal song that will touch the heart of any woman who has ever pursued her freedom from whatever malady that once held her captive. She has written this book in the spirit of *I Know Why the Caged Bird Sings*, the autobiography of one of the most prolific writers of our time, Maya Angelou.

Martica's voyage has been fraught with tears, trials and tribulations. Only through God's grace was she able to triumph. What would have caused many others to become another negative statistic is the very thing that caused her to be a revelatory beacon of truth.

Unconditional Love: One Woman's Journey to Spiritual Freedom is a spiritual handbook for the modern women that addresses the struggles, traps, and unrealistic expectancy that one may have as she journeys down the road of life in pursuit of freedom. This honest, transparent look into the mirror of

Martica's life may just help you find your true identity and the key to spiritual freedom. It's a must read for any woman who finds herself on the other side of her destiny to true liberation.

Who is Martica L. Offord-Sherman?

She is a passionate teacher sharing her life's experiences, a life coach mentoring with purpose, a serial entrepreneur, a mother and grandmother, a teacher of God's gospel of truth, and an advocate for the continued education for youth and young adults.

www.ingramcontent.com/pod-product-compliance
Lightning Source LLC
LaVergne TN
LVHW041549070426
835507LV00011B/1000